*Images of Modern America*

# MONTANA RAILS
## MOUNTAINS TO PRAIRIES

American railroads once commissioned posters encouraging travel. During the 1920s, the Northern Pacific Railway hired Vienna-trained artist Gustav Wilhelm Krollman to portray scenery along its line. Here, the *North Coast Limited* appears to fly by Emigrant Peak in the Paradise Valley—one of many scenic attractions that awaited passengers on a trip to Yellowstone National Park. (Author's collection.)

ON THE FRONT COVER: The snow-capped Crazy Mountains are a fine backdrop for Burlington Northern train No. 121, with "Tiger Stripe" No. 3131, traveling Montana Rail Link track at Mission Siding near Livingston on May 14, 1989. (Ed Lynch.)

UPPER BACK COVER: Amtrak's *Empire Builder* skirts the southern boundary of Glacier National Park. (Photograph by Dale Jones.)

LOWER BACK COVER (from left to right): Montana Rail Link on Winston Hill (photograph by Dale Jones), Milwaukee Road boxcabs (C.G. Heimerdinger Jr.), Burlington Northern Santa Fe (BNSF) at East Glacier Park (photograph by Dale Jones).

*Images of Modern America*

# MONTANA RAILS
## MOUNTAINS TO PRAIRIES

Dale W. Jones

ARCADIA
PUBLISHING

Published by Arcadia Publishing
Charleston, South Carolina

Printed in the United States of America

Library of Congress Control Number: 2019955538

For all general information, please contact Arcadia Publishing:
Telephone 843-853-2070
Fax 843-853-0044
E-mail sales@arcadiapublishing.com
For customer service and orders:
Toll-Free 1-888-313-2665

Visit us on the Internet at www.arcadiapublishing.com

*Here's to all the railroad men and women, past, present, and future, who keep the trains rolling through the mountains and prairies of Montana.*

# CONTENTS

# ACKNOWLEDGMENTS

On March 6, 2016, I received an e-mail that changed my path as an author. Since the year 2000, in addition to my Railroads of Montana website, I have self-published full-color Montana railroad calendars, three 28-page booklets, and two DVD books. Then, on that March day, an acquisitions editor for Arcadia Publishing contacted me wanting to know if I would be interested in working on a book about railroads in Montana. I had lived in Glacier National Park/Flathead Valley for many years, so naturally, my first book would be *The Great Northern Railway in Marias Pass*, followed up with *The Milwaukee Road Connection: Spokane to Butte*, and then *The Spokane International Railway*. This being my fourth book with Arcadia Publishing, I appreciate all the assistance I have received from the staff and a job well done to Stacia Bannerman, who has kept the projects moving forward. Once again, a special thank-you goes to railroad historian and master model railroad builder Jerry Quinn, who generously allowed me to peruse his Pacific Northwest photograph collection. Thanks go to the many individuals who reached out and shared their photographs and narratives, including Keith Blount, Chuck Bohi, Mark Demaline, William Edgar, Art Jacobson, Ed Lynch, Gary Ostlund, and Larry Zeutschel. After researching and accumulating railroad photographs and memorabilia for over 50 years, the original photographers' identities unfortunately may have become lost. If I have used your photograph without giving you credit—it is unintentional. Of course, heartfelt thanks to my wife, Bonnie, for her unfailing support throughout the years.

Unless otherwise noted, all photographs are by Dale Jones.

# INTRODUCTION

The mountains and prairies of Montana are the result of eons of geological time and millennia of human habitation. The routes railroads chose were influenced by ragged peaks, sandstone bluffs, flat-topped coulees, expansive valley prairies, and raging rivers. The human side of the story began thousands of years before Christopher Columbus's ships landed in the Bahamas. Nomadic ancestors of modern Native Americans may have hiked over a land bridge from Asia to what is now Alaska several ages ago. Through the centuries, the indigenous tribes engaged in sharing and trading with each other via a complex and far-reaching network of land trails and waterways. A key route along the eastern foothills of the Continental Divide was the Old North Trail. Walter McClintock in his 1910 work quotes a Blackfoot native: "There is a well-known trail we call the Old North Trail. It runs north and south along the Rocky Mountains. No one knows how long it has been used by the Indians. My father told me it originated in the migration of a great tribe of Indians from the distant north to the south, and all the tribes have, ever since, continued to follow in their tracks."

Prior to Lewis and Clark's Corps of Discovery, apparently few white men had visited the region. The first known to have explored this region was Sieur de La Vérendrye, who made his way up the Missouri River during the years 1730 to 1744, reaching the Rocky Mountains in January 1743. He did not remain, nor contribute any valuable historical information about the country.

Lewis and Clark recorded in detail their voyages of 1804 and 1805 up the Missouri River and the Clark Fork River, across the Bitterroot Mountains, and down the Columbia River to the Pacific Ocean, returning along the Yellowstone River. While Lewis and Clark were mapping the Missouri River drainage on the east side of the Continental Divide, Canadian surveyor David Thompson explored the west side of the divide including the Columbia River and its many tributaries. After Lewis and Clark and David Thompson presented their maps and geographic descriptions of the Montana region, it was not long before mountain men, fur trappers, and gold miners from both the United States and Canada entered Big Sky Country.

Throughout the early 1800s to the 1850s, an assortment of travelers and trappers located new trails and water routes through the interior of the Rocky Mountains. In 1862, gold was discovered in southwestern Montana along Grasshopper Creek, with boomtowns emerging in Bannack, Virginia City, and Helena. To protect and unite the distant Western lands, the first planned long-distance road, the Mullan Military Road, commenced construction in 1860 at Fort Benton on the Missouri River, terminating 661 miles to the west at Fort Walla Walla, Washington Territory. Today, Interstate 15 and Interstate 90 follow approximately the route of John Mullan's road through Montana, Idaho, and Washington. Through the 1850s to the 1870s, Montana was crisscrossed by numerous wagon roads; notable was the Corinne Road connecting Corinne, Utah, with Virginia City—this road would later become the path of Montana's first railroad, the Utah & Northern, completed to Butte on December 26, 1881. This route was later acquired by the Union Pacific.

Railroad building began in earnest during the 1880s. From a shaky start in 1870, the Northern Pacific Railroad was the first transcontinental railway in Montana, completed August 23, 1883, at Hell Gate Canyon, 55 miles west of Helena. A last spike ceremony was held on September 8 at Gold Creek; interestingly, this spike was the same one hammered down 13 years earlier at Thomsons Junction, Minnesota, on February 15, 1870. The Chicago, Burlington & Quincy (CB&Q) entered Montana south of Billings in the early 1900s.

Next in line across Montana was James J. Hill's Great Northern Railway. Hill purchased several St. Paul, Minnesota, bankrupt companies in 1878 and revitalized them until they were profitable. In 1879, under the corporate umbrella of the St. Paul, Minneapolis & Manitoba Railway (StPM&M), the road headed northwest out of the Twin Cities across North Dakota into Montana, reaching Great Falls on October 16, 1887. At Great Falls, the "Manitoba" connected with Jim Hill's Montana Central Railway awaiting construction through Helena to mineral-rich Butte in November 1888. In September 1889, Hill formed the Great Northern Railway, with the objective of reaching Puget Sound and the Pacific coast, but first the Great Northern needed to find a suitable route over the Continental Divide. For years, rumors had circulated about an easy pass over the mountains, but the Blackfeet and Salish tribes did not desire railroads cutting through their hunting grounds. They protected the location until late 1889, when an Indian guide took a Great Northern engineer named John F. (Frank) Stevens into the mountains and showed him the pass, now called Marias Pass, located south of Glacier National Park. At 5,213 feet in elevation, it proved to be the easiest of all passes used by the railroads to cross the Rockies.

The Montana railroad story continues into the early 20th century with two Johnny-come-lately railways. In 1909, the "Milwaukee Road," or the Chicago, Milwaukee, St. Paul & Pacific Railroad, entered Montana with "the Soo Line," officially the Minneapolis, St. Paul & Sault Ste. Marie Railroad, building into northeastern Montana around 1914. Since both lines basically shadowed existing routes built by the Great Northern and Northern Pacific, neither were particularly prosperous in Montana. Nearly all US rail companies suffered financial trauma during the Great Depression of the 1930s. The economic aftershock sent railroads scrambling to improve profits while attempting to maintain adequate services to shippers and residents. Ultimately, by the late 1960s, most railroads had to merge to remain solvent. The Burlington Northern Railroad fashioned from the Great Northern; Northern Pacific; Chicago, Burlington & Quincy (CB&Q); and the Spokane, Portland & Seattle (SP&S) in 1970 assimilated a large portion of Montana rail routes. The Milwaukee Road held out until 1980, when most of its Montana trackage was abandoned. The Montana Rail Link and Central Montana Rail were created in the mid-1980s to ease the threat of a Burlington Northern monopoly. This book examines railway operations from the 1970s through 2000 across the colorful mountains and prairies of the Big Sky State of Montana.

*One*

# RIVERS AND MOUNTAINS

If mountains are the backbone of Montana, then rivers are its lifeblood. Mountain ranges like the Beartooth, Bitterroot, Cabinet, Flathead, and Gallatin Mountains see the rivers Missouri, Kootenai, Bighorn, Powder, and Tongue zigzag through their slopes. Montana Rail Link SD45R No. 351 leads a westbound along the Flathead River in the Coeur d'Alene range near Perma.

In September 1997, Burlington Northern Santa Fe C44-9W No. 960 heads west at Kootenai Falls. Riverboat traffic on the Kootenai River was vital to mining camps and other development between Montana and Canada. In June 1899, a tragedy occurred as the river steamboat *Gwendolyn* was being transferred by flatcar west through Kootenai Falls to a new location. The *Libby Mountanian* of July 22, 1899, reported, "An accident occurred on a sharp curve . . . a shift to one side caused the boat to wrench itself loose from the moorage and fall off. To make matters, it fell over a fissure in the rocks in the canyon and fell to the bottom, fully 50 feet, turning over completely and lighting on the smokestack." Reportedly, parts of the boiler can still be seen at low water.

Dwarfed by Dancing Lady Mountain in Glacier National Park, an October 1993 eastbound *Empire Builder* No. 8 picks up speed after crossing the Two Medicine Bridge at East Glacier. The abrupt change from near vertical escarpments to level prairie influences the weather, triggering strong winds from the west and southwest. Some areas between Browning and Augusta have experienced winds of between 100 and 125 miles per hour. A Burlington Northern (BN) dispatcher recalls, "BN installed an anemometer at [Browning], because it was one of the more notorious locations for bad winds . . . a system was wired into the block signal system preset to turn the blocks red if a certain wind speed was attained, but a few years later in a high wind, the anemometer itself was blown over." (Ed Lynch.)

Where is the train? The construction of 422-foot-high Libby Dam on the Kootenai River necessitated building 57 miles of new roadbed and the seven-mile Flathead Tunnel for the Great Northern Railway. To continue rail operations, a shoofly track was constructed along the river with a 230-foot "tunnel through the dam." The October 24, 1970, eastbound *Western Star* is seen running through Libby Dam in the center of this photograph.

Construction on the Flathead Tunnel through Elk Mountain commenced at 3:00 p.m., September 30, 1966, with the final "holing out" at 11:10 a.m., June 21, 1968, by Pres. Lyndon Johnson. At "hole through," the horizontal error was .64 of a foot. Here, the eastbound Amtrak *Empire Builder* exits the north portal at Twin Meadows in the 1990s.

The northernmost point on the Burlington Northern Santa Fe follows the Kootenai River through a narrow 19-mile canyon between Yakt, Montana, and Crossport, Idaho. The railroad upgraded the line from Yakt to Troy, Montana, in 1999. On April 21, 1999, BNSF No. 1103 leads an eastbound into Troy on the new track alignment.

It is common practice for railroads to occasionally run unscheduled passenger trains. Here, on August 24, 2000, a westbound BNSF Special, led by GE C44-9W No. 4449, passes Radnor near Eureka. During the 1930s through the 1950s, the Great Northern contracted with a fish hatchery near here to provide fresh rainbow trout for travelers on the famous *Empire Builder*.

In the early 1800s, David Thompson became the first white man to explore, survey, and put northwest Montana on the map—literally. In 1809, Thompson followed a well-used trail along the Saleesh River (Clark Fork). The Northern Pacific Railroad built through this corridor in the 1880s; the photograph above highlights the rocky terrain along the Clark Fork. Below, three Burlington Northern GP39-2s scurry west of Thompson Falls where the Clark Fork River valley widens. (Above, Bruce Butler, Jerry Quinn collection; below, William Edgar.)

A spring 2000 cloudburst envelopes a Montana Rail Link (MRL) work train distributing new ties near Toole. The MRL is one of a few railroads in the United States that operates a "Jimbo"—the yellow crane-type contraption seen on top of the gondolas. The machine uses a boom to raise itself along the top edge of gondolas and hydraulics to slide across to the next car in a caterpillar fashion. Note caboose No. 1005. This is not a caboose in the usual sense—it is a "shoving platform." With the advancement of end-of-train (EOT) devices, cabooses slowly fell out of favor, and shoving platforms began to appear as a place to safely house a crew when a reverse move was required.

"The Moose is loose," reported the *Missoulian* of August 31, 2001: "This isn't a fire you just run in and put out," stated the fire team commander battling the Moose fire. Lightning sparked the Moose fire in Flathead National Forest on August 14 that swiftly grew to 71,000 acres. Behind westbound BNSF C44-9W No. 1014 is billowing smoke from the Moose fire. Below, Great Northern GP9 No. 733 is switching the small Belton (West Glacier) yard in August 1966. In the background are scars from the disastrous 1929 Half Moon fire. There has been a fire in Glacier National Park almost every year—with 1964 being an exception. (Below, Dale Jones collection.)

The Flathead Valley was not accessible from the east until 1890, when Great Northern contractors began building a supply road from Bad Rock Canyon to the summit of Marias Pass. In October 1989, ninety-nine years later, Burlington Northern No. 7118 and two Soo Line SD40-2s move westbound freight effortlessly through the canyon. (Jerry Quinn.)

After creation of Glacier National Park in 1910, the Great Northern launched extensive development programs. Maj. William R. Logan, superintendent, stated, "Develop the Park as rapidly as possible." In addition to hotels and chalets, the railroad positioned signs highlighting mountain peaks; here, BNSF No. 7302 passes the "Edwards" sign near Nyack.

Winters are long in northwest Montana; the cold season lasts from November 15 to February 28, with an average daily high temperature in the low 30s. Snowfalls can be substantial; during the winter of 1996–1997, Essex received a total accumulation of over 20 feet. Despite conditions, Montanans brace up and enjoy the weather. Above, skiers depart at Essex for world-class cross-country skiing. Below, the crew producing an advertising film for Amtrak in 1989 experienced the same blizzard conditions that John F. Stevens suffered 100 years earlier while locating Marias Pass for the Great Northern Railway.

Above, Jerry Quinn snaps a photograph of a fellow railfan filming the eastbound Amtrak *Empire Builder* at "False Summit" in Marias Pass. False Summit is exactly that—false. There is a westbound one-percent grade from Glacier Park to Bison; at Bison, the track alignment levels out near Lubec Lake before tackling a 1.2-percent westbound grade to the actual summit of Marias Pass in the distance. Below, an eastbound BNSF General Merchandise train of August 1999 glides by one of the many pothole lakes near False Summit. (Above, Jerry Quinn.)

During the autumn of 1889, John F. (Frank) Stevens traveled from the east to locate an acceptable route through Marias Pass, stumbling into the summit during a blizzard on December 10, 1889. Lesser known was C.F.B. Haskell's journey up the Flathead River and Bear Creek Canyon to the Marias Pass summit. Haskell wrote to his wife describing his trek: "My foot is pretty sore . . . I froze it the 3rd of Jan'y [1890] and afterwards walked over 100 miles on it. I should not have frozen it, but I wet it and was very anxious to reach the Summit . . . The day we were at the Summit Jan'y 5th was a beautiful clear day . . . How I longed for my camera to catch some of these glorious views." The author had his camera ready in August 1996 to document this eastbound Burlington Northern freight along Bear Creek.

In the photograph above, a 1990s-era westbound BNSF freight at Browning is juxtaposed behind a traditional Blackfoot ceremonial site. In July 1806, on the return trip from the West Coast, Meriwether Lewis left William Clark behind to explore the Marias River. The farther north the river went, the bigger the United States would be, as it marked the boundary of the Louisiana Purchase. Lewis hoped he would reach the 50th parallel—he did not, thus the name Camp Disappointment. Below, near Piegan and behind the haze of 20th-century diesel exhaust, a westbound BNSF train passes an obelisk marking the spot near Camp Disappointment.

While the Northern Pacific Railroad was building through Montana in 1873, a railroad military escort under Lt. Col. George Armstrong Custer was attacked by about 350 Sioux and Northern Cheyenne. Historian Barbara Fifer comments, "Winning this skirmish gave the colonel a deep, and ultimately deadly, belief that the Sioux and Cheyennes were 'cowardly' and one good charge was all it took to beat them." Custer learned in June 1876 at the Little Bighorn that the Sioux and Cheyenne were not cowards. The railway's last spike was driven at Gold Creek on September 8, 1883. A 1983 centennial celebration at Gold Creek included an 1861 Cooke steam locomotive. Below, the passenger train and the "local" at Drummond illustrates a typical scene from the 1960s. (Jerry Quinn collection.)

*Two*

# HEART OF THE PRAIRIE

The bluebird box on the MP (milepost) No. 37 telegraph pole has probably seen more avian activity than the original railroad branch line from Lewistown to Winnett. In the mid-1910s, the optimistic Milwaukee Road built north from Lewistown to Roy, Winifred, and Winnett, expecting revenue from agriculture and promising oil fields. Between 1972 and 1980, all the lines were abandoned as expenses outweighed profits.

Lewistown may be the heart of the prairie but not the exact center of Montana. For decades, there has been an ongoing controversy surrounding the precise location of Montana's center. The earliest story dates to 1912, when it was believed the heart of the state was under Mrs. Dockery's kitchen sink on Main Street. It was said, "You could look down the drain of Mrs. Dockery's sink and see the exact center of Montana." In 2006, Gerry Daumiller, a Montana geographic specialist, put the center in a Hutterite colony cow pasture at 109°38.3'W 47°1.9'N, eleven miles west of Lewistown. Above, in March 1996, BN GP38-2 No. 2313 waits at the old Milwaukee Road Lewistown depot (Yogo Inn); below, a BN train is at the former Great Northern station, converted to a gas station in the 1990s.

Two railroads served Lewistown: the Milwaukee Road north from Harlowton and the Great Northern Lewistown Branch from the Billings/Great Falls line. The optimistic expectations of the Milwaukee and Great Northern did not materialize, and by the 1960s, rail traffic had decreased with the bankrupt Milwaukee Road's last train leaving Lewistown on March 28, 1980. In the aftermath, Burlington Northern took over many abandoned segments of the Milwaukee Road; here, two BN trains pass through the heart of Lewistown neighborhoods. The photograph above has GP39M No. 2870 approaching a unique wigwag signal at Sixth Avenue South. In the spring of 1997, a flowering crabapple tree frames the BNSF No. 2745 train descending into Lewistown.

Only in Montana cattle country would a Burlington Northern employee open gates to let a train out of a pasture. On a gray March 1995 day, the Lewistown local is pulling some woodchip cars from the Berg Lumber Company spur west of town.

The lush green hills of the South Moccasin Mountains form an early morning backdrop as four BNSF GP39-2s attack the one-percent grade out of Lewistown in May 1997. Visible in the background is the 1937-era combination Great Northern/Milwaukee trackage from Spring Creek Junction to Lewistown.

Here, BNSF GP39-2 No. 2717 climbs westbound out of Lewistown. During the summer of 1928, the steep railroad grade into town caught the attention of some mischievous boys. The lads found a 10-pound can of grease and—thinking it would be great fun—applied a liberal coat of grease on the rails up the hill from Little Casino Creek until the grease ran out. Later that day, both the evening westbound freight and Harlowton bound passenger train headed up the hill but slid back into the yard. It took section hands several hours to clean the tracks with kerosene and mops. The boys suffered some remorse and confessed to the dastardly act and were "sentenced" to join the Boy Scouts and put up safety posters for the railroad every Saturday for a year.

A winter weather report for central Montana many times reads, "A fast moving arctic cold front swept into central Montana bringing with it a dramatic drop in temperatures and near whiteout conditions." One community event organizer remarked, "Our mountains are unique . . . Lewistown is nicknamed 'snowhole' because of how the mountains sit in a circular shape around our community." Above, a westbound local disappears into an April 1997 blizzard near the Lewistown cemetery. Below, a five-unit GP39-2–powered Lewistown local heads toward the Harvest States Elevator on the old Great Northern/Milwaukee dual trackage to Spring Creek Junction.

Central Montana is renowned for upland bird-hunting. Fergus County abounds with ring-necked pheasants, sage grouse, and Hungarian partridge. In the mid-1990s, the Burlington Northern, and later BNSF, ran special trains for select guests to Lewistown during regular bird-hunting season. In October 1995, Burlington Northern GP38-2 No. 2354 leads a westbound train near Glengarry.

The interior of the Great Northern Stanford depot captures the atmosphere of a small-town railroad station. Despite being ticket agent, baggage handler, and telegraph operator, one station agent described his primary duties as learning "the art of killing time while being lonely." Once passenger service was discontinued in 1966, responsibilities lessened until this station was demolished in 1996.

Burlington Northern Bicentennial SD40-2 No. 1876 and three other locomotives, including a cabless F7/9 "B" unit, are westbound near Garrison on October 15, 1978. Photographer Ed Lynch comments, "Fall colors and train makes a fine portrait of the BN in the late 1970s. This is one of the best photos I ever took!"

Two Burlington Northern GP38-2s lead the 1989 *Montana Centennial Special* through Wolf Creek Canyon near Wolf Creek. Beginning in Spokane with a specially painted Montana Rail Link locomotive, the train covered the MRL mainline to Livingston with trips up the branches to Polson and Darby. At Helena, the Burlington Northern took charge for the rest of the trip. (Ed Lynch.)

In the mid-1900s, the Great Northern and Milwaukee Road built through the heart of Montana, expecting revenues that never materialized. In 1997, this bumper wheat harvest is stored safely in industry-approved piles, awaiting loading at the junction of the former Great Northern/Lewistown line at Moccasin.

The timber grain elevator was a common North American prairie icon. Concerning the advantages of wooden grain elevators, one authority explains, "The wood walls are advantageous compared to the steel and concrete counterparts, because they actually absorb moisture from the grain." Burlington Northern SD40-2 No. 8068 westbound passes the elevator at Hobson.

The first major railroad into Central Montana was the Billings & Northern between Billings and Great Falls around 1908. This 225-mile rail line linked Chicago and the Midwest to the markets of Montana and the Pacific Northwest via the Chicago, Burlington & Quincy Railroad. Here, BN SD40-2 No. 8046 exits 1,131-foot Tunnel Q5 on the Great Falls/Billings line near Fife on September 5, 1990. (Ed Lynch.)

On the BNSF Laurel Subdivision, near the old Great Northern Railway siding of Wallum, a westbound freight with BNSF SD40-2 No. 7223 crosses Careless Creek trestle heading upgrade toward Great Falls on the Billings to Great Falls line in the summer of 1998.

# *Three*

# MILWAUKEE ROAD EAST

No locomotive epitomizes the Milwaukee Road's Montana electrification more than the "Little Joe." Prior to the 1950s Cold War, twenty 5,500-horsepower locomotives were built for Russia—as tensions rose, the deal fell through, and the Milwaukee purchased 12 units. Alluding to Russian leader Joseph Stalin, employees called them "Joe Stalins," later shortening the name to "Little Joe." No. E79 sits at Three Forks. (Jerry Quinn.)

C.G. Heimerdinger Jr. used Ektachrome Pro 2.25-by-2.25-inch color slide film to photograph the Milwaukee Road around Butte and Anaconda during the 1960s. The decades have produced a slight color shift, adding a warm patina to this image of No. E81—one of the four Milwaukee electric steeplecab switchers working here at Butte.

By the late 1970s, operations on the Milwaukee Road's Pacific Extension were crippled by slow orders and frequent major derailments. With revenues improving as a condition of the 1970 Burlington Northern merger, the railroad was able to continue its annual rail relay program. At Newcomb on Pipestone Pass, Nos. E73 and E21, with a five-unit boxcab helper, glide downgrade to Butte on the Fourth of July 1973. (Jerry Quinn.)

On June 3, 1973, No. E77 heads westward toward 2,290-foot Tunnel No. 11, cresting the Continental Divide at Pipestone Pass. This section of railroad was one of the first in the country to be electrified—it is said Thomas Edison came to ride across the mountains into Butte. (Jerry Quinn.)

In a holiday card setting, snow lingers at the Continental Divide summit of Pipestone Pass on March 11, 1973. Jerry Quinn caught this westbound freight with two Little Joes as they entered the east portal of Pipestone Pass Tunnel. (Jerry Quinn.)

An eastbound train with three-unit boxcab helper No. E45B, a Little Joe, and three GP40s exits Tunnel No. 11 in a billow of smoke. Helper engineer Fred Coombes chose the helper position until his retirement, stating his reason to work out of Butte as "I can sleep in my own bed every night." (Gary O. Ostlund.)

Milwaukee Road SD40-2 No. 162 with eastbound Tacoma, Washington, to Bensenville, Illinois, train No. 200 is at Donald on Pipestone Pass. In 90-degree weather in August 1979, the helper crew, positioned "up on the hill," uncouples its power from the head end to return to Butte. (Ed Lynch.)

The Chicago, Milwaukee, St. Paul & Pacific's crossing of the Continental Divide was built during 1909. The eastern entrance of the 2,290-foot Tunnel No. 11 under the summit was at an elevation of 6,347 feet, which made this the highest point on the Milwaukee Road. Historian Richard Gibson describes conditions surrounding the construction of the Pipestone Pass Tunnel in the April 28, 2019, *Anaconda Standard*: "The commissary at the headquarters camp provided tobacco, pipes, shoes, socks, underclothes, and other supplies, as well as abundant food and even a gallon of 'white pine syrup,' a cold remedy." This image of No. 25 blasting out of the east portal of Tunnel No. 11 was taken by renowned railroad photographer Doug Harrop. Harrop passed away in 2014; longtime friend Bruce Kelly recalled, "He could tell true tales of the rails better than most, and back it all up with stellar photographs taken both lineside and from the cab." (Doug Harrop, Ed Lynch collection.)

Little Joe No. E78 and three SD40-2s cross the Blacktail Viaduct westbound toward Butte in September 1973. Milwaukee Road trestles were unusual in that they were designed to sway without lateral or longitudinal braces, while most railroad trestles are more rigid.

In this unusual perspective at Grace Siding, the green-lighted signal indicates clear track ahead, but deferred maintenance is taking its toll on what was once the fastest track from Chicago to Tacoma. In a year, the catenary and the electrics would be history, and by March 1980, the track would see trains no more. (Gary O. Ostlund.)

On the east side of Pipestone Pass was an awe-inspiring mountain grade and horseshoe curve called the Vendome Loop; here, No. E21 trudges up the "Loop" near Cedric on the 22-mile grueling two-percent grade from Piedmont to the summit of Pipestone Pass. The peaks in the background are part of the Tobacco Root Mountains. (Jerry Quinn.)

Despite concessions for additional freight traffic after the Burlington Northern merger in 1970, by March 1973, the Milwaukee generally ran only four through trains a day, with every second or third day running what was called a "dead freight." These trains generally had two Little Joes and two diesels performing work along the division. (Jerry Quinn.)

After electrified operations ended in 1974, the Milwaukee Road tried to eliminate manned helper operations, which required an extra crew, with Locotrol, an early form of remote control where the engineer of the lead locomotive could also operate the mid-train units. As track conditions deteriorated through the financial difficulties of the 1970s, transit times increased, leading to a return to manned helper operations. This Milwaukee Road westbound freight at Vendome with No. 18 on the point is just starting up the grade to the Continental Divide at Pipestone Pass. (Wayne Monger.)

On March 11, 1973, Little Joes Nos. E21 and E78 hug the rock escarpment near Trident. The Gallatin, Jefferson, and Madison Rivers come together here forming the mighty Missouri River. Interestingly, Sacagawea, a young Native American woman, was taken captive at the Missouri River headwaters and returned with the Lewis and Clark Expedition as an interpreter and guide in 1805. (Jerry Quinn.)

A Milwest historical group inspects the Eagle's Nest Tunnel in Sixteen Mile Canyon near Lombard in August 1989. The route through the canyon covered several miles including the Eagle Nest Tunnel and a 300-foot bridge crossing Sixteen Mile Creek. The west portal, seen here, featured a standard concrete approach abutment. (Jerry Quinn.)

On an August 1976 afternoon, two empty gondolas and a quaint 1940s-vintage Milwaukee Road SW1 No. 873 work the leased White Sulphur Springs and Yellowstone Park Railway. John Ringling of Barnum & Bailey Circus fame built the 22-mile line from Ringling to White Sulphur Hot Springs to winter range his animals. (Clyde Parent, Jerry Quinn collection.)

Two Joes and two diesels with a westbound freight attack the heavy grade from Bruno to Loweth in May 1974. The hills and prairies of Montana are quite verdant in May and June until the unrelenting heat of July and August turn the greens to browns. (Jerry Quinn collection.)

Harlowton, or "Harlo" for short, was named for Richard Harlow, builder of the Montana Railroad. Harlowton was the eastern end of the Milwaukee Road's 440-mile Montana based electrification terminating at Avery, Idaho. Harlowton was also a center for steam and electric locomotive shops and servicing facilities. No. E57B, seen here working the yard at Harlo, was one of a handful of boxcabs assigned as single unit ES-3 switchers; today, it is preserved and on display in downtown Harlowton. (Above, Jerry Quinn collection; below, Matthew Herson Jr., Jerry Quinn collection.)

Within a month, there would be no Milwaukee Road trains running through Washington, Idaho, and most of Montana. The last revenue Nos. 200 and 201 moved across steel rails one last time during the first week of March 1980. This meet of Nos. 200 and 201 at the west switch Newcomb near Butte on a bitter February 8, 1980, morning was a harbinger of things to come. (Ed Lynch.)

Leased Butte, Anaconda & Pacific GP9 No. 106 works the Milwaukee Road Harlowton Yard on February 19, 1979. In one year almost to the day, the last train would leave Harlo during the last week of March 1980 for the last time. (Ed Lynch.)

As deferred maintenance took its toll on the right-of-way, the Milwaukee experienced numerous derailments in the final months leading up to the 1980 embargo. Here, train No. 800, with SD10s Nos. 558 and 553 and SD9 No. 522, backs into Great Falls Yard after a June 16, 1979, detour on the Burlington Northern. (Ed Lynch.)

Rarus Railway took over the former Butte, Anaconda & Pacific Railway on May 1, 1985. It was electrified from 1913 to 1967; with the road's first diesels, seven GP7/9s delivered in the 1950s. Here, three Rarus/BA&P units work back to Garrison from Butte in Durant Canyon in April 1988. (Ed Lynch.)

45

This photograph illustrates that Central Montana is prone to severe winter snowstorms. Milwaukee Road FP7 No. 97-C and SD10 No. 558 with cut widener (snowplow) No. 900036 stop to use the phone at Judith Gap on the Lewistown/Harlowton line. They will work up to Moore and pick up another unit, then plow back to Harlo. (Ed Lynch.)

Harlowton was not only a terminal for Milwaukee Road electrics, but also a service facility for steam and diesel locomotives. Milwaukee GP20 No. 975 gets some maintenance inside the Harlowton roundhouse on May 5, 1979. Photographer Ed Lynch relates, "In the last days of Lines West, employees were friendly to visiting railfans wanting photographs. That's how I got in."

# *Four*

# CENTRAL MONTANA RAIL

Central Montana Rail Inc. is an 84-mile short line through Judith Basin, Fergus, and Chouteau Counties. Much of the CMR track between Kingston to Geraldine was built by the Milwaukee Road, with a 20-mile connection from Kingston to the BNSF at Moccasin. In July 1996, the *Charlie Russell Chew-Choo* dinner train crosses the 1,698-foot Sage Creek Trestle.

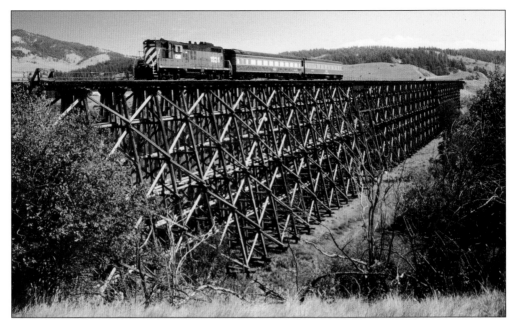

Created in 1985 as a freight only railroad, in 1994, the Lewistown Chamber of Commerce initiated a "Wild West" dinner train called the *Charlie Russell Chew-Choo*. During the first two years, the *Chew-Choo* ran with railcars painted in the Southern Pacific (SP) "Daylight" scheme. These two photographs feature both the SP passenger cars and the Spring Creek Trestle. This 1,391-foot-long, 78-foot-high wooden trestle was built in 1912–1913 by the Great Northern (GN). Unique was a gauntlet arrangement, whereas both the GN and Milwaukee Road physically had two sets of tracks across the bridge, being switched at either end to align movements to or from Lewistown on their respective rails.

The former Milwaukee Road Lewistown–to–Great Falls rail line encountered large valleys to bridge, several grades to climb, and the boring of six tunnels. A few miles west of Kingston/ Spring Creek Junction, the 1997 version of the *Chew-Choo* crosses the first of three spectacular steel and concrete viaducts. The Judith River trestle is a 33-span bridge roughly 150 feet high and the longest on the line, measuring in at 1,953 feet. The five stainless-steel Budd Rail Diesel Cars (RDC) on this train were acquired in 1996 by the Lewistown Chamber of Commerce from the North Shore Scenic Railroad in Duluth, Minnesota.

There is a saying in Montana: "If you don't like the weather, then wait twenty minutes and it will change altogether." These two trains were photographed in early summer on the 1,303-foot-long Indian Creek Trestle between Ware and Danvers. The photograph above from June 17, 1995, has Central Montana Rail GP9 No. 1810, with two leased Northwest Rail Museum passenger cars on a pleasant 89-degree afternoon. Below, on June 22, 1996, almost one year to the day, No. 1810 is leading four of the newly attained Budd RDC cars with the Denton bound *Chew-Choo* on the heels of an afternoon thunderstorm that brought winds over 20 miles per hour and a quarter inch of rain.

The 2,014-foot Sage Creek Tunnel, known locally as the "Hoosac Tunnel," is bored through unstable shale, hardpan, and solid rock. The tunnel required over a year of near-constant work to complete, making it the largest single project on the Milwaukee Road Lewistown–to–Great Falls line. Exiting the tunnel is CMR No. 1810 with the August 1997 westbound *Chew-Choo*.

The *Charlie Russell Chew-Choo* runs an annual December "North Pole Express" offering visitors the opportunity to experience a Central Montana winter landscape. In December 1997, the westbound train is passing the forgotten town of Hoosac. In its heyday, there were two elevators, a railroad depot, general store, post office, school, and saloon. Nothing is left today except an ancient grain elevator and a few abandoned buildings.

After the Milwaukee Road abandoned the Pacific Extension in 1980, Burlington Northern purchased what was left of the railroad in Central Montana. "We're going to rebuild the Lewistown-Geraldine line," BN officials stated; by 1983, the railroad had abandoned 67 miles from Hanover to Geraldine. To continue rail service, Central Montana Rail was created in 1984. The BN delivered five GP9 locomotives, a caboose, and this office/maintenance building at Denton.

In 1912, the Great Northern built the Moccasin-to-Lewistown branch. Today, Central Montana Rail (CMR) operates the 20-mile Kingston to BNSF connection at Moccasin. In 1995, CMR No. 1810 heads back to Denton past Kolin's last grain elevator—in 2020, the elevator is gone and only a few abandoned buildings remain.

Central Montana Rail ships mostly wheat, but the summer of 1996 saw an unusual movement—steel pipeline pipe. The Express Pipeline System was authorized to build a 1,717-mile oil pipeline from Hardisty, Alberta, to Casper, Wyoming. In the photograph above, CMR GP9s Nos. 1838 and 1814 swelter in the 93-degree July heat at Coffee Creek before heading down the Arrow Creek Breaks to Geraldine. The Arrow Creek Breaks were a curse to the railroad as unstable soils triggered numerous landslides. Below, at Pownal, a westbound "pipe train" passes a "rock train" heading up the mountain with fill rock to stabilize the sagging right-of-way.

Central Montana landscapes and lifestyles are immortalized in the paintings of Charles Marion Russell, commonly known as Charlie Russell, the "Cowboy Artist." One of Russell's more recognizable canvasses, titled "When the Land Belonged to God," includes a scene with Square Butte in the background—but which Square Butte? There are apparently 11 Square Buttes in Montana. The landmark in the Russell painting is the Square Butte above the cab of CMR No. 1838 near the town appropriately named Square Butte. Like Charlie Russell, Central Montana Rail reflects the individuality and tenacity that makes Montana Montana.

*Five*

# ENGINE NO. 261

Each year since 1996, BNSF Railway has chosen a variety of locations across its network offering train rides to employees and invited guests. In August 1998, on a tour of the Midwest, the Burlington Northern Santa Fe Appreciation Special was powered by Milwaukee Road 4-8-4 No. 261, the largest operating coal-burning steam locomotive in North America.

On August 16, 1998, No. 261, with a BNSF SD70MAC as supplemental motive power, pulls the 16-car BNSF Special from Snowden toward Glendive along the Yellowstone River. Note that three cars back from the diesel locomotive is a HEP (head-end-power) car essential to suppling passenger cars electrical power.

Steaming west (geographical south) at 40 miles per hour on the BNSF Sidney Line Subdivision, No. 261 passes the small switching yard at Sidney, Montana. An "oil local," seen on the far-right track, is led by GP38-2, former Conrail No. 7983 and now No. 783, painted in the corporate blue-and-white General Motors color scheme.

Milwaukee Road No. 261 is a 4-8-4 "Northern-type" steam locomotive, built in 1944 by the American Locomotive Company (ALCO) in Schenectady, New York. It was used for both mainline freight and passenger service until retired around 1954. Capable of running at high speeds, on Sunday, August 16, 1998, the No. 261 clocked 60 miles per hour between Terry and Miles City.

Milwaukee Road's 1910s advertising literature declared, "No one need fear the winters of Montana. The summer days are long and although at midday the sun is quite hot, sunstrokes are unknown." On a hot August 1998 afternoon, Milwaukee Road No. 261 challenges the hype while traveling through unproductive sagebrush on both sides of the track near Fallon.

Forsyth made headline news 100 years prior to August 16, 1998, when this BNSF Special arrived in town. In April 1894, Jacob Coxey initiated a "March on Washington," protesting the failure of government action in solving the unemployment crisis stemming from the Panic of 1893. On April 21, 1894, some 300 men, led by out-of-work Butte teamster William Hogan, commandeered a Northern Pacific train in Butte and headed for Washington, DC, where they planned to join "Coxey's Army." The stolen train sped across the state with the law in hot pursuit. They were finally apprehended in Forsyth on April 25. Above, Milwaukee Road No. 261 arrives in town on August 16; below, No. 261 departs eastbound in the golden glow of a Monday, August 17 morning.

On the return trip east, the 1998 BNSF Employee Appreciation Special hugs the banks of the Yellowstone River at Kamm, near Terry. During the 1870s and 1880s, steamboats plied the waters of the Yellowstone from Fort Union on the North Dakota border to Billings, Montana; upon completion of the Northern Pacific in 1883, the need for steamboat travel slowly disappeared.

Attacking the one-percent grade up Beaver Hill east of Glendive, the 1998 BNSF Employee Appreciation Special leaves Montana near the Makoshika State Park "badlands." The landscape offers an array of different features of hogback ridges, pinnacles, and fossil remains of Tyrannosaurus Rex and Triceratops.

On the evening of August 16, 1998, Milwaukee Road No. 261 slumbers with a big Howdy Hotel sign in the background. Local pioneer Hiram Marcyes built the hotel using bricks from his own brickyard. The primary purpose of the business, which was first called the Commercial Hotel, was catering to railroad passengers and crews. During a wave of Old West nostalgia in the early 1950s, the Commercial Hotel was renamed the Howdy Hotel after becoming the winning entry in a local contest.

# *Six*

# MONTANA RAIL LINK

Montana Rail Link was created in 1987 when Missoula businessman Dennis Washington leased Burlington Northern's (former Northern Pacific) southern Montana route between Huntley, Montana, and Sandpoint, Idaho. MRL received the nickname "Milwaukee Road Lives" from usage of GP9s and antiquated semaphore signals, as seen here at Toole in October 2001.

Montana Rail Link is considered a mid-sized, class II railroad. At its start-up in October 1987, MRL purchased a total of 52 locomotives from Burlington Northern. Since then, the railroad has acquired many used locomotives. In a June 1998 rainstorm, No. 600, a former Duluth, Missabe & Iron Range SD9, sits at Paradise.

Paradise, Montana, was established in 1883 with construction of the Northern Pacific (NP). The former NP depot is still used by Montana Rail Link as a yard office and signal maintainer's storehouse. Here, MRL GP9 No. 107 runs around a Montana Rockies Rail Tours excursion train returning to Missoula.

At Thompson Falls in June 1993, GP9 No. 115 is pictured with a weed spray train that targets thistles or knapweed that sprout along the right-of-way. Why the red dots on MRL locomotives? One version is somebody had a red dot laying around when they were painting the first unit, and the wife of MRL president Dennis Washington liked it.

On a foggy October 2001 morning, the westbound MRL "gas local" crosses the Jocko River Bridge at Arlee. The gas local runs from Missoula to the delivery station at Pipeline near Thompson Falls. In 1995, the Yellowstone Pipeline was permanently shut down for safety reasons; today, the gas local links the eastern and western segments of the existing pipeline.

Montana Rockies Rail Tours operated excursion trains in the Mountain West from 2001 through 2005. The tours of October 2001 ran a circle route of MRL's Clark Fork line through St. Regis, returning on the Paradise/Evaro Hill 10th Subdivision. Bringing up the rear along the Flathead River near Perma is Wisconsin Southern Railroad's *Northern View.*

Montana Rail Link gas locals have reached cult status due to regular scheduling and easy access for photographs. Gas locals usually leave Missoula early morning and early evening, 12 hours apart, seven days a week. This gas local on the 10th Subdivision parallels Highways 93 and 200 from Missoula to Paradise. On the return trip, trains travel along Interstate 90 via the 4th Subdivision route from Paradise to Missoula.

On Sunday, October 21, 2001, the Montana Rockies Rail Tours excursion glides along the smooth waters of the lower Flathead River about 10 miles east of Paradise. Now operated by Montana Rail Link, this was the original Northern Pacific route over Evaro Hill. The grade up Evaro Hill is handicapped by 2.2-percent grades in both directions and a lack of sidings. The "River Line" along the Clark Fork was built from Missoula to Wallace, Idaho, in 1893 and extended from St. Regis to Paradise around 1908. While traffic over this line was slow due to its twisting, river-hugging nature, the new route gave the Northern Pacific a line free of major grades.

The eastbound October 2001 Montana Rockies Rail Tours passes beneath the Northern Pacific–era signal bridges at Desmet. Traffic patterns vary, but the original NP 1883 north route veering off to the right faces the 2.2-percent mountain grade over Evaro Hill; as a rule, the south Clark Fork River route via St. Regis is the preferred path.

Montana Rail Link's corporate headquarters are in Missoula along with the business car fleet and engine servicing facilities. Looking south from the Northside Missoula Railroad Historic District pedestrian bridge, the diesel fuel servicing station and locomotive storage can be seen in the background.

Looking west from atop Tunnel No. 5.5, the cottonwood trees along the Clark Fork River near Alberton appear to glow in the October 2001 afternoon sun as a Montana Rockies Rail Tours excursion, led by MRL GP9 No. 107, heads east back to Missoula from Paradise.

Montana Rail Link GP9 No. 105 is crossing a trestle south of Charlo on the Polson Branch. Built for the Northern Pacific in 1957 as No. 318, MRL No. 105 has been renumbered many times until 2008, when the Southern Railway of British Columbia designated it No. 135. (Kirk Petty, Jerry Quinn collection.)

Montana Rail Link's Mullan Pass crosses the Rocky Mountains near Helena on the old Northern Pacific route. This short section of railroad has two horseshoe curves, two spectacular trestles, and the famous Mullan Tunnel. In the photograph above, an eastbound freight approaches the west portal of the tunnel at Blossburg. When originally constructed in 1883, the 3,896-foot tunnel was less than 13 feet wide, making it one of the narrowest tunnels in the country. In 2009, the tunnel was enlarged five feet taller and three feet wider to accommodate today's large freight trains and protect locomotives from overheating as they push through the mountain. Below, westbound trains pull a two-percent uphill grade through the tunnel, creating a billow of locomotive exhaust when existing the bore. (Both, Jerry Quinn)

There are two tall curved trestles on Mullan Pass. The NP designated the lower crossing over Greenhorn Creek the Greenhorn Creek Viaduct and the upper crossing over Austin Creek originally as the Austin Creek Viaduct but more commonly known by locals as the Skyline Trestle. Six Burlington Northern locomotives of mixed heritage lead a westbound over Austin Creek Trestle on July 5, 1991. (DL Zeutschel, Jerry Quinn collection.)

The clock marks 7:00 p.m. while MRL SD45-2 No. 322 waits at the 1900s vintage Northern Pacific Helena depot. While comparing NP Montana depots, one railfan remarked, "Of the four brick depots in Montana, that include Livingston, Billings, Helena and Missoula, personally, I like Helena because it's the only one with a clocktower, which still works by the way."

In the early 1880s, the Northern Pacific constructed a major steam engine repair facility at Livingston. After the Burlington Northern merger in 1970, the railroad assigned diesel rebuilding to other shops, closing the Livingston works in 1985. The Livingston Rebuild Center reopened the shop in 1988. Here, a hodgepodge of locomotives await rebuilding in August 1989. (Jerry Quinn.)

The freight cars trailing behind this westbound train are barely visible, which emphasizes the steep upgrade between Townsend and Winston, known as Winston Hill. The track profile shows it as nine miles of continuous nearly one-percent grade. One locomotive engineer explains, "Once the train loses momentum, it's a long slow grind . . . it's the curves that get us."

The first commercial cement plant in Montana at Trident produced cement for many large-scale projects, including Fort Peck and Grand Coulee Dams. On July 13, 1991, an eastbound MRL freight passes the cement production complex. (DL Zeutschel, Jerry Quinn collection.)

Montana Rail Link GP9 No. 119 switches at Billings Yard next to Pandrol Jackson Rail Grinder No. RMS-13. Rail grinders were developed to increase the lifespan of the rails by removing deformations and corrosion. The RMS-13 power unit was originally built as Pennsylvania Reading Seashore GP38 No. 2001 in 1967; thirty years later, in 1997, there had been a complete external transformation, as seen here.

On August 11, 1991, a westbound freight, led by three Burlington Northern SD40-2s, twists and turns along the rugged Missouri River canyon near Lombard. On July 25, 1805, Meriwether Lewis surveyed the Missouri River in this area and wrote that he "observed that the rocks which form the clifts on this part of the river appear as if they had been undermined by the river and by their weight had separated from the parent hill and tumbled on their sides." (DL Zeutschel, Jerry Quinn collection.)

*Seven*

# Hi-Line

What is the "Hi-Line?" The Hi-Line is the section of US Highway 2 between the Rocky Mountain front in Montana to the North Dakota border on the east. Near the beginning of the Hi-Line at Cut Bank, eastbound Amtrak *Empire Builder* No. 8 sprints across the Cut Bank Creek Trestle on August 19, 1999.

The jagged peaks of the Two Medicine Valley in Glacier National Park loom in the background as Amtrak locomotive GE Dash-8 P40B No. 800 with the eastbound *Empire Builder* enter the Hi-Line from Marias Pass at Piegan in the winter of 1997.

Cut Bank touts itself as the "Coldest Spot in the Nation," ignoring Alaska, of course. The September 27, 1979, afternoon temperature is much warmer at 72 degrees Fahrenheit as this unusual mix of locomotives, including a Burlington Northern GP30, a Milwaukee Road SD40-2, and a Grand Trunk SD40, wait to move westward. For the record, the town of Stanley, Idaho, is often the coldest place in the lower 48. (Ed Lynch.)

The Canadian Pacific Railway reaches into Montana at the Sweetgrass, Montana–Coutts, Alberta, border north of Shelby. In this 1986 scene, SD40-2 No. 5832, sporting white "extra" flags, has retrieved freight cars from a westbound Burlington Northern train parked on the Montana side earlier that morning.

Some of the most perfect "horizons" on the Hi-Line can be found between Blackfoot and Shelby. Here, a BNSF grain train glistens in the early morning prairie sun near Ethridge. These 100-car trains of Greenbrier Gunderson 5,188-cubic-foot covered hopper cars are painted in a "worm-brown" color, earning these trains the moniker "Earthworm."

Burlington Northern Santa Fe GE Dash 9-44CW No. 1101 and Conrail Blue GE Dash 8-40C No. 6028 lead a westbound unit grain train through the big "S" curves a few miles west of Shelby at MP 1065.4 on the Hi-Line Subdivision.

This sign along US Highway 2 points to Shelby and Havre. The Great Northern Railway set the blueprint for development of northern Montana as it platted nearly all the towns and even selected familiar European city names to entice settlers—Glasgow, Malta, Zurich, Kremlin, and Harlem to name a few.

Charles F. Martin founded the Fraternal Order of Empire Builders in 1973 to preserve everything related to the Great Northern Railway. In 1982, the name was changed to the Great Northern Railway Historical Society (GNRHS). The 1998 GNRHS annual convention in Great Falls sponsored this group touring Shelby—no railfan event is complete without a photo op.

In October 1890, the Great Falls & Canada three-foot-gauge railroad from Lethbridge, Alberta, to Great Falls reached a half-way point called Virden. The Great Northern intersected the line, renaming the town Shelby. Here, arriving from Great Falls in June 1999, GP50 No. 3125 changes crew in Shelby.

Dunkirk, nine miles east of Shelby, is an inconspicuous dot on the map. One travel writer remarked, "The unincorporated town of Dunkirk is one of those classic 'blink and you miss it' kinds of places. At 70mph, if you close your eyes and count to 2, you'll miss the downtown. It's a grain elevator and across the street, the Frontier Bar and behind it, a house. That's it." The town may not have much to offer, but for train watchers, the two dozen or more trains a day, like westbound Dash-9 C44-9W No. 983, are enough reason to stop and look around.

The vagaries of weather and economic conditions doomed many Hi-Line towns as the years passed. Full of promise in the 1890s, Galata today is nearly a ghost town, as seen by the leaning time-worn St. Anthony & Dakota Elevator as the westbound *Empire Builder* whizzes through town in August 1996.

The Great Northern station pictured here at Hingham is a typical example of dozens of GN depots throughout Montana. It was a standard-plan structure, 30 by 48 feet, located on the north side of the main track with a passing siding and one or more industry tracks for shippers of bulk commodities. (Author's collection.)

After the Great Northern; Northern Pacific; Chicago, Burlington & Quincy (CB&Q); and Spokane, Portland & Seattle (SP&S) merger of March 1970, the newly formed Burlington Northern Railroad entered the "Rainbow Daze" period of multicolored locomotive and passenger train colors from predecessor railroads. In early 1970, former CB&Q E8 No. 9941 leads a colorful *Empire Builder* east to Chicago. (Jerry Quinn.)

A few miles west of North Dakota and officially leaving the Hi-Line, BNSF SD40-2 No. 6819 takes the main line through Snowden. The tracks in the foreground lead to the Snowden Lift Bridge, constructed by the Great Northern around 1913. An interesting side note—vehicles shared the bridge from 1916 until 1986.

*Eight*

# YELLOWSTONE RIVER COUNTRY

From its headwaters in Yellowstone Lake downstream 670 miles to the Missouri River in North Dakota, the Yellowstone River is one of the last free-flowing rivers in the lower 48 states. The area is rich in Native American history and natural resource development; here, Burlington Northern GE C30-7 No. 5585 follows the Little Bighorn River with a unit coal train.

Located in a remote area of southwest Montana, Virginia City sprang to life in 1863 after gold was discovered in nearby Alder Gulch. When the gold ran out a few years later, Virginia City was left frozen in time. In 1964, local entrepreneur Charlie Bovey dreamed of building a tourist railroad from Virginia City. Eventually, the 30-inch narrow-gauge Alder Gulch Shortline was built on a 1.5-mile loop powered by a restored 2-8-0 No. 12 purchased from the Escanaba & Lake Superior Railroad. Unfortunately, No. 12 went out of service in 2010. Sometimes criticized for his unorthodox approach to acquisition and preservation of historic buildings, one commentator remarked, "This was Charlie's whole life . . . He wasn't interested in making money by preserving history. He was interested in preserving history."

On an overcast May 1999 day, three varieties of Electric Motive Division (EMD) SD (six-axle Special Duty) locomotives await duties at Glendive yard. From left to right are Oakway Leasing SD60 No. 9059 with a standard cab, BN SD60M No. 9235 featuring the three-piece windshield nicknamed "triclops," and the energy efficient wide-cab 4,000-horsepower AC-traction drive BNSF SD70MAC No. 9997.

On May 14, 1989, Burlington Northern train No. 121, the Birmingham Portland Express, with Tiger Stripe GP50 No. 3131, is heading west on Montana Rail Link trackage at Mission Siding near Livingston. The snow-capped Crazy Mountains are a fine backdrop on this beautiful spring day. (Ed Lynch.)

A GE 44-ton switcher of unknown heritage scuttles tank cars at a railcar cleaning facility in Miles City. The train in this September 1997 photograph is working on one of the few remnants of Milwaukee Road main line rails in Eastern Montana.

In 1954, the Northern Pacific introduced dome cars to its flagship passenger train, advertising it as the *Vista-Dome North Coast Limited*. One employee remembers, "Four domes required about 12 minutes—or about 3 minutes to clean per car. When that train left Livingston, all the dome windows were very clean." (Jerry Quinn.)

When Amtrak officially took control in May 1971, the majority of US long-distance passenger train service was in disarray. Across the country, passenger train itineraries were cut, with Montana in the crosshairs. Amtrak discontinued the former Northern Pacific route across southern Montana, which serviced most of the state's population centers. After pressure from Montana senator Mike Mansfield, the carrier instituted the *North Coast Hiawatha* (*NCH*) on NP's main line through North Dakota and Montana in June 1971. Ridership on the *NCH* was favorable, but funding and confusing alternating-day schedules plagued the train until it was discontinued October 1, 1979. Above, westbound Amtrak No. 9 passes a Burlington Northern freight near Bozeman in May 1974, below, the *NCH* rests at Bozeman. (Above, Jerry Quinn; below, author's collection.)

In April 1967, the Jerry Quinn family completed a cross-country trip from the East, culminating their western journey on Northern Pacific's *North Coast Limited* (*NCL*). The above photograph shows Pullman Sleeper No. 369 being serviced at Billings. This 1967 westbound *NCL* 10-car train included one baggage car, two coaches, dome, coach, dome, sleeper, dining car, dome-sleeper, and finally the last sleeper; Jerry recalls, "We were in this last car." In the photograph below, snow clings to the hills as *North Coast Limited* No. 25 enters the east entrance of the Bozeman Tunnel. Passengers in the last dome car have a clear view as Northern Pacific officials insisted dome cars be separated by at least one "flat top" car, so front row dome passengers had less obstruction to forward vision. (Both, Jerry Quinn.)

Homestake Pass near Butte was a treasure to railfans; the distinctive granite rocks were just as unique as the mixed Burlington Northern and Amtrak passenger cars on Northern Pacific's *North Coast Limited* and short-lived Amtrak *North Coast Hiawatha*. The Homestake Pass Line, running from Garrison to Logan via Butte and Homestake Pass, was built in 1888 by the Northern Pacific. The June 1974 photograph above has westbound Amtrak *North Coast Hiawatha* at the summit of Homestake Pass. Photographer Gary O. Ostlund says of the image above, "The *North Coast Limited* was arguably the most beautiful train in the world," adding, "the pic almost looks like an HO layout." (Above, Gary O. Ostlund; below, William Edgar.)

In the spring of 1972, five Great Northern long-nose forward GP20s lead the daily Butte–Great Falls freight upgrade out of Butte to Elk Park Pass. The GN line from Great Falls through Helena to Butte was built with assistance from mining magnate Marcus Daly to stifle Northern Pacific and Union Pacific domination of rail transportation in and out of Butte. (Gary O. Ostlund.)

A subsidiary company of the Union Pacific (UP) Railroad took control of the original Utah & Northern line from southern Idaho to Butte in 1889. On August 23, 1980, train No. 278 heads westbound (geographical south) near Melrose over UP's Montana Division on its way back to Pocatello, Idaho, after picking up cars at Silverbow/Butte. (Ed Lynch.)

# *Nine*

# WHERE IS PLENTYWOOD?

Many folks are unaware of the 150-mile Great Northern Railway line north from Bainville to Plentywood/Scobey/Opheim near the Saskatchewan border or the Soo Line's 57-mile Montana portion of the Whitetail Subdivision. On former Soo Line trackage, Dakota, Missouri Valley & Western's No. 316 approaches the end of the line at Whitetail.

Prior to Great Northern Railway's entrance into northeast Montana around 1910, it is reputed that Butch Cassidy aided rustlers to move stolen cattle across the border on "the Outlaw Trail." In less dramatic circumstances, BNSF GP38 No. 2140 will soon leave historic Plentywood eastbound on January 6, 2000.

In October 1999, BNSF GP38-2R No. 2183 eases downgrade from Flaxville to Redstone. Large letters on hillsides were common throughout the West. Historian James J. Parsons notes, "Hillside symbols can be traced . . . to a single decade, 1905–1915. Once built, letters became symbols of community and school . . . shouting, 'Here we are!' " It appears Redstone's "R" needs attention.

The Soo Line Whitetail Branch pushed into Montana from Flaxton, North Dakota, promoting settlements along the way. The town Dooley was plotted along the line in 1913 with grand expectations, only to survive into the 1960s. In August 1998, a Dakota, Missouri Valley & Western (DMVW) train to Whitetail passes the Rocky Valley Lutheran Church, one of the last buildings standing in Dooley.

The 57-mile portion of the former Soo Line trackage from Westby to Whitetail had a 10-mile-per-hour speed limit. Considering the poor condition of the right-of-way, it will take this 30-car DMVW westbound about 30 minutes to travel the half mile to Raymond.

The undulating roadbed stretching out behind No. 316 is near a short-lived settlement west of Outlook named Daleview. An amusing anecdote transpired here in 1923, when Elmer E. "Hominy" Thompson, thinking the Soo Line owed him compensation for crossing his land, moved a neighbor's barn onto the tracks, stopping trains—unfortunately, he did not get the desired results and was arrested for interfering with US Mail service.

The town of Outlook was promoted as "being surrounded by some of the finest agricultural sections to be found anywhere, farmed by men of the highest standard type." Here, DMVW No. 316 stops at the Outlook depot. The Soo Line's original intent was to make Outlook a division point on the failed ambition of a northern route reaching Great Falls.

"HELL NIGHT! Third of Outlook is Devoured by Fire," was the bold headline from the *Billings Gazette* of November 2, 1999. Outlook was just one casualty of several devastating fires that burned in eastern Montana on Halloween, October 31, 1999. Outlook fire chief Scott Wangrin remarked, "The fire started about 1:30 p.m. Strong winds, at times gusting so heavily that they blew gravel, like hail, sweeping the fire into Outlook." There is speculation that perhaps the DMVW train sitting here may have started the fire. The *Gazette* reported, "A Sheridan County deputy stopped the train in town Sunday afternoon to prevent it from starting any more grass fires." In addition to having two locomotives destroyed, the fire burned two wooden trestles, warped rails, and scarred right-of-way.

After the two Dakota, Missouri Valley & Western locomotives were destroyed in the Outlook fire, GP35s Nos. 862 and 865 took over running trains from Westby to Whitetail. On a snowy winter afternoon, a 24-car train of empty grain cars is shuttled into Whitetail and returned loaded to the Canadian Pacific Railway connection at Flaxton, North Dakota.

On March 10, 1914, the western extremity of the Soo Line was completed to Whitetail. The company had hopes of building farther west into Montana, but the realities of cost versus return slowed growth. Here, DMVW No. 316 slowly approaches the end-of-road for the Soo Line Whitetail Branch—688 miles west of headquarters at the Minneapolis, Minnesota, Shoreham Shops.

Montana is a contrast of old and new, vibrant and sepia, mountains and prairies. This Montana sheepherder, while preserving traditions of millennia, watches the 1998 Burlington Northern Santa Fe Employee Appreciation Special roll by as the 21st century nears. The late summer scene is a study of brown and sage, whereas spring brings bright yellow balsamroot and pastel rose-colored bitterroot, the Montana state flower. The railroads of Montana have a history as large as the Big Sky and remain an important figure in the state's future development. Whether shiny rails are traversing Native American trails or spanning level plains and timbered mountains, trains will continue to cross the Montana landscape. From the first narrow-gauge steam engine that rolled into Montana Territory in 1880 to Montana Rail Link's EMD SD70Ace and Burlington Northern Santa Fe's General Electric ES44C4 diesel locomotives, the future is secure—trains will continue to move over Montana rails from mountains to prairies.

# DISCOVER THOUSANDS OF LOCAL HISTORY BOOKS
## FEATURING MILLIONS OF VINTAGE IMAGES

Arcadia Publishing, the leading local history publisher in the United States, is committed to making history accessible and meaningful through publishing books that celebrate and preserve the heritage of America's people and places.

Find more books like this at
## www.arcadiapublishing.com

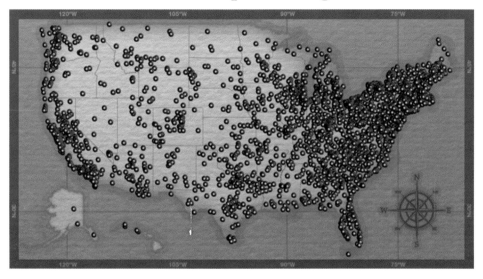

Search for your hometown history, your old stomping grounds, and even your favorite sports team.

Consistent with our mission to preserve history on a local level, this book was printed in South Carolina on American-made paper and manufactured entirely in the United States. Products carrying the accredited Forest Stewardship Council (FSC) label are printed on 100 percent FSC-certified paper.

MADE IN THE USA